P H Emerson

PHOTOGRAPHER OF NORFOLK

A portrait of Dr P. H. Emerson, B.A., M.B. (Cantab.), M.R.C.S. Eng., A.K.C., Fellow of the Royal Horticultural, Meteorological and Photographic Societies and member of the Society of Arts. The portrait is from the obverse of an Emerson Medal.

Peter Turner and Richard Wood

P H Emerson

PHOTOGRAPHER OF NORFOLK

DAVID R. GODINE · BOSTON

David R. Godine   Publisher
Boston, Massachusetts

LCC 74–81518
ISBN 0–87923–106–8

Printed in Great Britain by Westerham Press, Westerham, Kent
Designed by Peter Guy

Contents

List of Illustrations in the Text

Acknowledgements

In gathering material for a book such as this, it is necessary to use many sources. To all those who have helped us we extend our most sincere thanks. In particular, for their invaluable assistance, we would like to thank Gail Buckland and Leo de Freitas of the Royal Photographic Society; C. S. Middleton; William Jenkins of the International Museum of Photography at George Eastman House; Mark Haworth-Booth of the Victoria and Albert Museum; and, finally, James Fraser, whose enthusiasm for the project was as great as our own, and whose good advice assisted us in completing the book.

All the photographs in the section of plates are reproduced directly from originals in the Coleman and Rye Libraries of Local History, Norwich, and we are particularly grateful to Philip Hepworth, city librarian of Norwich, for making these originals available to us.

Emerson on the Focus Question

THE REASON we prefer pictures which are not too bright lies in the fact that the eye cannot look long at very bright paintings without tiring. As a physical fact, too, the most delicate modelling and tonality is to be obtained in a medium light. From what has been previously said, it will now be understood that a picture should not be quite sharply focussed in any part, for then it becomes false; it should be made just *as sharp as the eye sees it and no sharper*, for it must be remembered the eye does not see things as sharply as the photographic lens, for the eye has the faults due to dispersion, spherical aberration, astigmatism, aërial turbidity, blind spot, and beyond twenty feet it does not adjust perfectly for the different planes. All these slight imperfections make the eye's visions more imperfect than that of the optician's lens, even when objects in one plane only are sharply focussed, therefore, except in very rare cases, which will be touched upon elsewhere, the chief point of interest should be slightly—very slightly—out of focus, while all things, out of the plane of the principal object, it is perfectly obvious, from what has been said, should also be slightly out of focus, not to the extent of producing *destruction of structure* or fuzziness, but sufficiently to keep them back and in place. For, as we have been told, "to look at anything means to place the eye in such a position that the image of the object falls on the small region of perfectly clear vision, . . . and . . . whatever we want to see, we look at, and see it accurately; what we do not look at, we do not, as a rule, care for at the moment, and so do not notice how imperfectly we see it." Such is the case, as has been shown, for when we fix our sight on the principal object or *motif* of a picture, binocular vision represents clearly by direct vision only the parts of the picture delineated on the points of sight. The rule in focussing, therefore, should be, focus for the principal object of the picture, but all else must not be sharp; and even that principal object must not be as perfectly sharp as the optical lens will make it. It will be said, but in nature the eye wanders up and down the landscape, and so gathers up the impressions, and all the landscape in turn appears sharp. But a picture is not "all the landscape," it should be seen at a certain distance—the focal length of the lens used, as a rule, and the observer, to look at it thoughtfully, *if it be a picture*, will settle on a principal object, and dwell upon it, and when he tires of this, he will want to gather up *suggestions* of the rest of the picture. If it be a commonplace photograph taken with a wide-angle lens, say, of a stretch of scenery of equal value, as are most photographic landscapes, of course the eye will have nothing to settle thoughtfully upon, and will wander about, and finally go away dissatisfied. But such a photograph is no work of art, and not worthy of discussion here. Hence it is obvious that panoramic effects are not suitable for art, and the angle of view included in a picture should never be large. It might be argued from this, that Pseudo-Impressionists who paint the horse's head and top of a hansom cab are correct, since the eye can only see clearly a very small portion of the field of view at once. We assert, no, for if we look in a casual way at a hansom cab in the streets, we only see *directly* the head of the horse and the top of the cab, yet, indirectly, that is, in the retinal circle around the *fovea centralis* we have far more suggestion and feeling of horse's legs than the eccentricities of the Pseudo-Impressionist school give us, for in that part of the retinal field indirect vision aids us. The field of indirect vision must be *suggested* in a picture, but subordinated. But we shall go into this matter later on, here we only wish to establish our principles on a scientific basis. Afterwards, in treating of art questions, we shall simply give our advice, presuming the student has already studied the scientific data on which that advice is based. All good art has its scientific basis. Sir Thomas Lawrence said, "Painting is a science, and should be pursued as an inquiry into the laws of nature. Why, then, may not landscape painting be considered as a branch of natural philosophy, of which pictures are but experiments?"

Some writers who have never taken the trouble to understand even these points, have held that we admitted fuzziness in photography. Such persons are labouring under a great misconception; we have nothing whatever to do with any "fuzzy school." Fuzziness, to us, means *destruction of structure*. We do advocate broad suggestions of organic structure, which is a very different thing from destruction, although, there may at times be occasions in which patches of "fuzziness" will help the picture, yet these are rare indeed, and it would be very difficult for any one to show us many such patches in our published plates. We have, then nothing to do with "fuzziness," unless by the term is meant that broad and ample generalization of detail, so necessary to artistic work. We would remind these writers that it is always fairer to read an author's writings than to read the stupid constructions put upon them by untrained persons.

P. H. EMERSON, *Naturalistic Photography,* 1889

Introduction

DR. PETER HENRY EMERSON was an extraordinary man and is deserving of far more than an historical account of his activities in the world of late Victorian photography. Some understanding of what he was like as a person is essential to appreciate what he did, and what he did not, do for photography. Emerson was clear thinking, highly intelligent, logical and had an enormous capacity for hard work. He also epitomised our stereotype of the Victorian gentleman, for he was rich with independent means, arrogant, insufferably patronising to all he considered beneath him and selectively condescending to those whom he had to accept as his equals.

'To be a man of but one idea, or one accomplishment, is a very sorry distinction', wrote the topographical photographer Francis Frith and Emerson echoed these words by his deeds: he was a doctor of medicine, a naturalist, a photographer, a superb billiards player, a member of the Royal Meteorological Society and a writer of as yet unpublished detective stories. He was the author of no less than thirteen books as well as innumerable articles and lectures. Everything he did he approached with daunting vigour and investigated in obsessional detail, from his early days to his eightieth year.

Emerson must be regarded as one of the most important influences not only on late Victorian photography but also on the evolution of photography thereafter. As well as bringing direct pressure to bear on the photographic establishment through his own writing and photography, by recognising and encouraging talent in other photographers he began a chain of events which radically altered the course of photography. Alfred Steiglitz, ultimately responsible for the acceptance of photography as a valid means of expression and a fine art in America, was first recognised by Emerson, who awarded him first prize in a competition. Julia Margaret Cameron, whose striking portraits of Victorian notables are thought of today as photography at its most eloquent, was regarded as a photographic crank by many of her contemporaries. Emerson produced a book of her work and wrote a long essay in praise of her unconventional photographs while constantly advising his followers to study her pictures and gain inspiration from them.

The contemporary photographic milieu into which Emerson plunged himself was in a state of confusion for, in the rush to gain acceptance for the medium, its unique qualities were forgotten as Victorian artist/photographers sought to emulate contemporary painters. Photographs had taken on the appearance of 'works of art' by the use of chemicals to break down hard edges and through the production of composite prints telling moral tales in allegorical form. When the discovery of photography had been announced in 1839 far-sighted observers had predicted the ultimate death of painting; forty years later, prominent photographers, cap in hand, were begging to be considered as second-rate painters. However, a pioneering spirit began to grow amongst the more imaginative who saw the immense potential of photography in its own right and of these Emerson was the most vociferous and articulate. Almost single-handed he championed a new aesthetic and fought for the recognition of photography as a unique and independent fine art.

The ripples caused by Emerson's brief submersion in the photographic world spread wide, but in this book we have attempted to place his photography and his radical views only in their immediate context and to present his struggle to realise photography's great potential. We believe that the sixty-five photographs reproduced in the section of plates speak eloquently on their own for Emerson's eminence as a photographer whose pictures are not simply of historical interest but also continue to vindicate his championship of the photograph as a work of art.

Peter Turner
Richard Wood
NORFOLK
NOVEMBER 1973

P. H. Emerson

PETER HENRY EMERSON was born in 1856 in Cuba of an American father and an English mother. His father, a wealthy man, owned the La Palma Estate where the family lived until Emerson was eight when they returned to Massachusetts, their original home. After a short period in America Emerson senior died and the family returned to Cuba. Soon afterwards they left for England to escape the war that was developing between Spain and its colony. Once in England Emerson was dispatched to the recently founded Cranleigh School in Surrey. A natural scholar, he eventually went to King's College, Cambridge, where, according to contemporary reports: 'Besides having a brilliant record as a student of medicine, he edited the college magazine, led the college football teams to victory and was foremost in every outdoor sport and indoor studies, even gaining, to the utter bewilderment of his friends, the Leathes Theological Prize.'[1] In 1882 his first book was published, a picture of medical student life in London, it was entitled *Paul Ray at the Hospital*. In 1885, at the age of twenty-nine, Emerson became an F.R.C.S.

Besides pursuing a medical career Emerson had become involved in photography. His initial encounter with the medium came through his interest in ornithology, as he recognised photography as the obvious means of efficiently recording the facts necessary to further knowledge in this sphere. He bought photographic equipment in 1881 and was instructed in its use by E. Griffiths. His first serious use of photography was on an ornithological expedition in 1882 with his friend A. H. Evans, but whether the resulting photographs were successful or not has not been recorded. However, in the autumn of that year Emerson joined the Photographic Society of Great Britain and exhibited in Bond Street for the first time, gaining sufficient encouragement to provide the impetus for a deeper involvement in photography.

Typically, Emerson approached his new interest with enormous energy, studying not only the science and existing traditions of the medium but also examining the history of art in great detail, seeking a reasoned platform for his own rather unorthodox attitude, based on an admiration for the dedication of the 'naturalistic' school of painters and his feeling that photography offered a unique potential in recording truth. Emerson's scientific training as a doctor, coupled with his interest in the arts, led him to the realisation that photography was the medium where the merging of art and science took on the greatest significance. This field of investigation formed the kernel of his work during the following decade.

Coincident with this he began to crystallise his theories through the production of images that attempted to replace the artificiality and sugar-sweet sentiment he found in the 'pictorial' pictures of his contemporaries with a truer, more analytical expression based on his newly acquired understanding of the history of art. Emerson's assessment of the existing situation was that fine art appreciation was based on that most elusive, illogical and suspect of qualities – taste. Worse still, that taste was being dictated by a few irrational critics like Ruskin, who seemed to Emerson to be promoting an art that was merely decorative. It soon became obvious to him that photography had suffered greatly as a result of this unfortunate misunderstanding and he resolved to find a more rational basis from which to formulate his artistic philosophy.

During the time spent on these researches, Emerson moved to South-wold in Suffolk where he befriended a little-known but highly articulate painter of the 'naturalistic' school, Thomas F. Goodall. Goodall's under-standing of the relationship that existed between photography and the other visual arts seemed a touchstone in Emerson's development as a photographer and together they worked on a portfolio of pictures, *Life and Landscape on the Norfolk Broads*, which combined photographs of the wild sweeping East Anglian landscape with documentary style studies of the farm labourers and marsh men at work. The pictures, published in 1886 by Sampson-Low as a limited edition platinotype portfolio with a text by Goodall, were markedly different from those currently held to be examples of good photography; direct and honest, albeit in a rather romantic fashion, they seemed incongruous against the posed, contrived efforts of the 'high pictorialists', who dominated the English scene.

With this body of work behind him, Emerson decided to abandon his medical career. His growing, if controversial, reputation in photographic circles, topped by his success in publication, and coupled with a sizable private income, led him to forsake the chance of a possible fortune as a fashionable doctor, and take up the fight to establish photography as a unique medium at the forefront of contemporary art. Satisfied in his own mind that the Norfolk pictures proved beyond all doubt that a photograph direct from nature was infinitely superior to the elaborate constructions of the medium's leading figure, Henry Peach Robinson, Emerson began to lecture to the many photographic societies that were springing up through-out England. His aim was to propagate the theories that had been applied during the Norfolk Broads project, based on a combination of belief in photography as the logical partner to the 'naturalistic' school of painting, and in the power of the photographic medium as a fine art when used scientifically to capture the spirit of nature in all her moods and atmo-spheres.

His talks met with some success and early in 1886 he was elected to represent the interests of amateur photographers within the Council of the Photographic Society. During March that year Emerson, now thirty years old, delivered two lectures, both so controversial as to be reported in *The Amateur Photographer*. The first of these talks 'Photography a Pictorial Art' was read before the Camera Club in London, and in it Emerson attempted to explain why photography was a fine art:

> ... the painter strives ... to render, by any means in his power, as true an impression of any picture which he wishes to express as possible. A photographic artist strives for the same end, and in two points only does he fall short of the painter – in colour and in ability to render so accurately the relative values, although this is, to a great extent, com-pensated for by the tone of the picture. I here use the word in its artistic sense, and not in its misused photographic sense ... there is (also) ample room for selection, judgement and posing, and in a word, in capable hands, a finished photograph is a work of Art.... But we must

not forget that nine-tenths of photographs are no more works of art than the chromos, lithos, and bad paintings which adorn the numerous shops and galleries.[2]

Although the talk was considered controversial in some aspects, particularly his dogmatic approach to art criticism and the work of H. P. Robinson whom he described as a 'wiseacre', it seemed to an audience unwilling to change their views that Emerson was merely reinforcing the currently held opinion that a photograph should ape a painting to be successful. Realising his error, the next lecture Emerson gave set out at great length his hypothosis on what was and what was not great art. To a packed room at the Priory Hall, Great Yarmouth, he explained the futility of 'the *prettiest* water colours in all their meretricious pinks, blues, greens and false lights'. He attacked the 'daubs in oil of well-behaved dogs, wooden horses, theatrical shepherds, tin sheep, red fields, all painted with an outline and rigidity that would delight a stencil-plate worker.'[3] Art was enslaved Emerson argued, except when the artist went to Nature for his subject matter.

The clever Dutch painters were the first to get a true inkling – Hobbema, Ruysdael and others went to nature, but they were trammelled by conventionality and went in for beautifying nature – a rather dangerous experiment. In England, John Constable struck aside and studied nature but not with his whole soul. A few of his works went to Paris and were much admired. Rousseau followed in Constable's steps; all honour to the man; he formed an epoch. Then came Corot . . . then Jean François Millet . . . Bastein le Page. From such as these a whole host of

Angelus (1858–9) by J. F. Millet. Louvre, Paris.

In the Vineyard by J. F. Millet. Of those Emerson cited in his lectures and publications as 'great artists' none was so loudly praised as Jean François Millet: 'Let the student seize every chance of studying his works . . . here is a directness of expression never surpassed.' Museum of Fine Arts, Boston.

men in France, England and America have learnt their lesson. Many of these are living – aye, starving – in cottages, in huts, or boathouses studying nature, painting her truly not for the pictures sake only, but because they love her. . . . By photography can be expressed more truthfully and beautifully the beauties of nature than by any other black and white process – the drawing of the lens is unequalled, the tones of a platinotype print are perfect.[4]

The road to fine art is simple Emerson told his audience: know nature and you will recognise that which is good, patronise the artist, banish bad art – if you cannot afford a good painting, buy a good photograph.

Despite the passion of his talk, Emerson's succinct appraisal of the true road to photography as a fine art passed almost unnoticed – a brief flurry of

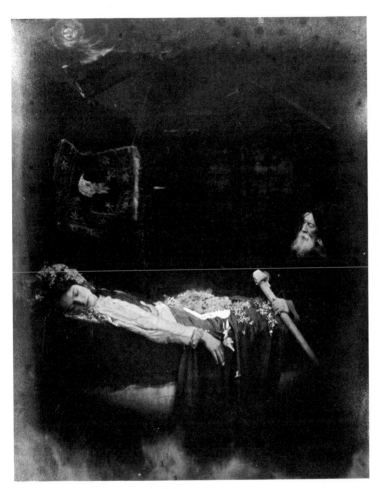 

of photography, and, realising that his pictures were well received even though his theories were rejected, he decided that he must make some more concrete opposition to Robinson and his followers.

Having further established his reputation with two fine portfolios, complete with descriptive text, *Pictures from Life in Field and Fen* and *Pictures of East Anglian Life* which were published as gravures in 1888 as the culmination of eighteen months work, he decided that he too would write a book, a handbook on photography that would instruct the would-be photographer in all that was necessary to produce photographs from nature, pictures that would stand in their own right as examples of fine art. In the years that had elapsed since his first attempts at propagating his ideals, Emerson had built upon his theories until now, he felt, he could safely provide unarguable scientific evidence to show the truth of his philosophy, and the weakness of the oil daubing, image manipulating antics of his fellow photographers.

Work on *Naturalistic Photography* began in 1888 and the book was published by Sampson-Low the following year. Its effect on the photographic establishment was shattering, for in stressing an honest and straightforward approach Emerson had swept aside decades of misdirection. A large part of the book was devoted to technical matters, explaining at length his views on the control of photography to render any scene from nature in the way that it was perceived by the photographer, thus to truly represent the scene in an artistic manner. His approach was rigorous, there was no place in naturalistic photography for the dilettante and there were many aphorisms, written to guide the beginner in a proper philosophic approach to his art. The technical advice stressed simplicity so that the photographer's full attention could be given over to producing his picture. The reader was advised to develop his negatives the day they were taken 'whilst yet the mental impression of what you are trying for is fresh' and enlarging and retouching, both currently popular in the creation of the combination prints Emerson disliked were firmly put down as 'the process by which a good, bad, or indifferent photograph is converted into a bad drawing or painting.'

In the book Emerson essentially reassessed the relationship between art and photography, bursting upon the photographic world with a set of ideas not new in themselves, but never before applied to photography. His starting point was that the best in art had always been drawn from nature's resources and had represented man's impression of these resources. In the same chapter he rushed through over two thousand years of art history to show how, at each stage of man's development, the best works of art have always been those which represent the true facts of nature as seen and felt by the artist. He stated how painters of the 'naturalistic' school were the first to fully comprehend the sensory reaction of the eye and brain, thus producing works that were fully 'truthful' and not merely accurately representative of the scene they depicted. His knowledge of the history of art seems to have been derived from the work of Woltmann and Woermann though the conclusions he drew from their studies were largely his own.

Beginning his treatise with a long chapter entitled 'Naturalism in Pictorial and Glyptic Art' it would not do Emerson justice to use any but his own words:

Nature is so full of surprises that, all things considered, she is best painted as she is. Aristotle of old called poetry an imitative art, and we do not think anyone has ever given a better definition of poetry, though the word imitative must not in our present state of knowledge be used rigidly. The poetry is all in nature, all pathos and tragedy is in nature and only wants finding and tearing forth.[6]

By Naturalism it will be seen that we mean a very different thing from realism. The realist makes no analysis, he is satisfied with the moats and leaves out the sunbeam. He will, in so far as he is able, paint all the veins on the leaves as they really are, and not as they LOOK as a whole. For example, the realist, if painting a tree a hundred yards off, would not strive to render the tree as it appears to him from where he is sitting, but he would probably gather leaves off the tree and place them before him, and paint as they looked within twelve inches of his eyes, and as the Modern Pre-Raphaelites did, he might even imitate the local colour* of the things themselves. Whereas the naturalist painter would care for none of these things, he would endeavour to render the impression of the tree

*A specific term used by Emerson to denote the colour of objects as they appear in the existing lighting.

taken as it appeared to him standing a hundred yards off, the tree taken as a whole, and as it looked, modified, as it would be by various phenomena and accidental circumstances. The naturalist's work we should call true to nature. The realist's work we should call false to nature. The work of the realist would do well for a botany class but not for a picture, there is no scope for fine art in realism, realism belongs to the province of science.[7]

He cites, for example, the granite lions outside the British Museum.

The lions, which are remarkable for strength of character and truthfulness of impression, may be taken as representative of the greatest period of Egyptian art. . . . They are hewn from granite, or porphyry, the hardest of stones, they have conventional moustaches, and are lying in conventional positions, yet withal, there is a wonderful expression of life and reserved strength about them which makes you respect them, stone though they be; and they convey to you, as you look on their long lithe flanks so broadly and simply treated, the truthful impression of strong and merciless animals.[8]

Emerson supported all this with a scientific analysis of the actual way in which we see nature (based on *Physiological Optics* by Hermann von Helmholtz) and he considered the many factors which contribute to our perception of reality; perspective, form, changes of colour with varying lighting, binocular vision, distance, etc. He concluded that it is therefore impossible to make a copy of nature in a two-dimensional image as, say, the Pre-Raphaelites had attempted to do, instead, one can only make a transcript – naturalistic art therefore represented a much closer approximation to our perception. In this way he attempted to establish a scientific basis for art. He next proceeded to level these arguments at existing photography with considerable force.

Emerson's incisive, if at times pompous, text presented the medium in an altogether radical manner. 'Do not call yourself an "artist photographer"' he instructed the reader 'and make "artist-painters" and "artist-sculptors" laugh: call yourself a photographer and wait for artists to call you brother.' 'No-one should take up photography who is not content to work hard and study so that he can take pictures for his eye only. The artist works to record the beauties of nature, the bagman works to please the public or for filthy lucre or for metal medals.'[9] Remarks such as these, aimed one feels with a certain malicious accuracy, fell hard upon Robinson and his disciples, but even harder for them to bear were Emerson's attempts to relate art and science. While he argued that the fundamental distinctions between the two disciplines were great, their areas of similarity were being too easily confused – optical sharpness in a photograph was being mistaken as a synonym for truth, the scientific principles which control the chemistry of the medium were becoming its *raison d'être* and the artificiality which springs from a subjugation of nature by a strictly scientific rendering of that which is before the camera was a poor and meaningless substitute for honesty, true emotion and art.

The chief opposition continued to come from Robinson and their differences were exaggerated by the fact that fashion had followed Robinson

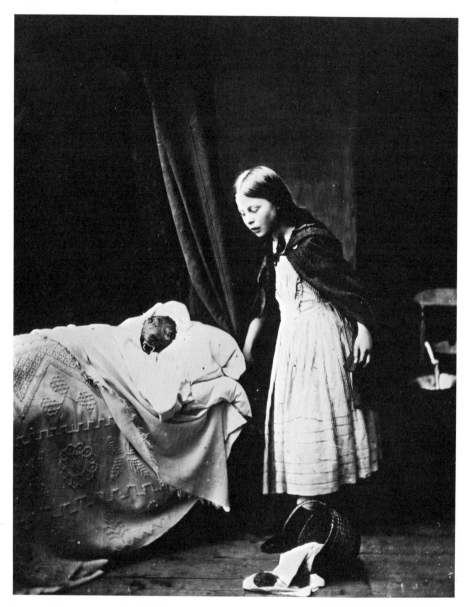

Red Riding Hood (1858) by H. P. Robinson. A fine example of the type of photograph Emerson despised. Reproduced by courtesy of the Victoria and Albert Museum, London.

since the 1860s. One point which became central to the controversy was the degree to which photography was able to interpret the real situation, for Robinson considered that interpretation necessitated no less than constructing images from fragments; infusing the straight truth with artificiality under the guise of imagination in an attempt to make the end product coincide as nearly as possible with some preconceived idea. His final images were saturated with typical Victorian sentimentality. Emerson's contention was that the artistic validity of the image rested entirely upon the selection of source material and the way in which it was treated.

According to his theory of naturalistic vision there was one factor which he particularly considered in depth; that in order to approach the feeling of human vision the principal part of the subject should be the only part in sharp focus, all else being subjugated to it. The remainder of the image, he stated, should be off sharp to a degree depending upon its distance in front, behind or to the periphery of the central object. He modified this by saying that in real life even the main object is never perceived with an utterly sharp outline. 'Nothing in nature has a hard outline . . . its outlines fade gently into that something else . . . (and) in this mingled decision and indecision, this lost and found, lies all the charm and mystery of nature.' This point, however, had been made with a qualifying paragraph warning against fuzziness being taken too far 'to the length of destroying the structure of any object, otherwise it becomes noticeable, and by attracting the eye detracts from the general and is then just as harmful as excessive sharpness. . . .'[10] (We hasten to add that this is what Emerson advocated. His photographs do not necessarily bear this out. A point never satisfactorily explained, or, indeed, ever referred to, is that throwing one plane out of focus inevitably requires that another be thrown into focus.) The question of sharp or soft was the concept most readily grasped by his enemies and discussions on the book frequently degenerated into an extended bickering over fuzzy against sharp. When *Naturalistic Photography* appeared, reviews were published in the photographic press. The *Photographic News* seemed heartily in favour of the book recommending it as 'a work which should be possessed and read by everyone interested in the practice of photography'.[11] But the editor of *The Amateur Photographer* recognising its controversial possibilities quickly seized the opportunity and handed a copy over to H. P. Robinson who launched a long and bitter, but anonymous, attack against all Emerson's principles – particularly against the theory that he put forward on focusing.

Robinson, accusing Emerson of wilful ignorance of the true facts, claimed that Art can give prominence to the important parts of the picture 'without any of these dodges', and generally dismissed his ideas as an excuse for trying to pass off bad photography as good art, a disease, Robinson claimed that must be halted. Emerson completely outraged by this onslaught from his rival wrote a long and angry letter to the editor of the *Photographic News*:

My Book *Naturalistic Photography* appeared and the erudite (!) and polished (!) editor gave it to Mr H. P. Robinson to review – at least so I am informed on good authority, though one would not like to believe it for Mr Robinson's sake, for one fondly hopes that there still lingers amongst us that nice sense of honour which prevents a *gentleman* from *anonymously* reviewing the work of an opponent. . . . This review appeared. It showed ignorance unbelievable and was wilfully and stupidly malicious. . . .

This delightfully ignorant critic proceeds to say that the naturalists 'wilfully ignore the fact that the eye changes its focus so automatically and instantaneously to adapt itself to vision that we are not conscious of it.' Indeed! And when did the critic become an authority in physiology? But the fact remains that I do not wilfully ignore the fact; vide *Naturalistic Photography*, pages 119, 120, which proves either that the reviewer did not read the book, in which case he was dishonest in his capacity as a reviewer or that he read and wilfully suppressed my remarks, in which case he was doubly dishonest as a critic and as a man. From this false premise, a creation of the reviewer's own brain, follow several specious deductions which are, of course, of no account.

So imperfectly educated does this reviewer appear to be, that he sees no difference between principles and rules. I do not guarantee to supply my readers with brains but only with food for good brains. Part of my remarks on composition are speciously suppressed . . . this is an archaic reviewer's game . . . with no more proof of what he calls the falsity of my doctrine than this sort of thing, he, with crocodile's tears, writes that it is his solemn duty 'to protect the young photographer from false doctrine that may be prejudiced to him, in the exercise of his art.'

My doctrines are called all sorts of names, but no proof is given to support the review, and the *Amateur Photographer* sets up as a disinfectant. The *Amateur Photographer* must not forget that disinfectants misapplied are poisonous, and so I regard that paper. The superior tone of this reviewer is a huge joke when you consider the ignorance he displays of all the aims and workings of modern art. A painter . . . on reading the review said, with a roar of laughter, 'why the fellow is an ignorant fool!' So much for the review and for the veracity of the reviewer.[12]

Inevitably, the following week, a reply appeared from Robinson, who curiously did not attempt to defend his critique, but simply rebuked Emerson for his 'hysterical scream'. However, Robinson was not content to let the matter lie, to another of his books *Picture Making by Photography* being reprinted at the time, he added a chapter specifically condemning Emerson's heresy on focusing as a retrograde step pushing photography back to the dark ages and saying that naturalistic photography could never last, as it was not 'true art'.

When the new edition appeared two months later, this condemnation was quoted at length in the *British Journal of Photography* a trade paper that had previously given *Naturalistic Photography* a poor review. By this time, Emerson's theories had gained numerous adherents, and one of these, Graham Balfour wrote in support of the new champion, saying that his theories were misunderstood and stating the case for differential focus, backing his argument, as Emerson had done, with the names of painters who subdued unimportant detail. In reply, Robinson issued a challenge – let Dr Emerson and his followers exhibit their works alongside his own, let their 'peculiar doctrines' be seen in practice. But Balfour was not to be so easily led. Had not Mr Robinson already seen Dr Emerson's pictures, he asked, had he seen none of the exhibitions at Pall Mall (the annual show-place for photography organised by the Photographic Society of Great Britain) which, for the past six years had displayed Emerson's prints? Could it be that Mr Robinson was fighting his battle from a position of total ignorance? And, in any case, as both men were leaders of their respective schools who could judge the contest? The only judge, suggested Balfour, could be time, and the adoption of one philosophy or the other by 'the best artists among photographers'. 'Is it to be equal focus', he asked 'dressed up models, combination printing and silver printing reluctantly abandoned or long patient study of tone and photogravure, that will win the day?'[13]

The correspondence continued to and fro, soon joined by letters from George Davison another prominent amateur photographer, and follower of Emerson, who patiently explained that the naturalistic photography did not, as was apparently supposed by its detractors, rest on Emerson's theory of focusing, but rather on 'Truth, and the best of everything'. By October 1889, matters had risen to a head, and Davison, who was then as forceful a champion of the new School as Emerson himself, wrote a long and concerned letter to the *British Journal of Photography*:

> Although Mr Robinson has ventured to add a chapter in a new edition of one of his books on the subject of *Naturalistic Photography* and presumably knows what has been going on in the world of pictorial art, he is still crying to know what naturalistic photography really is. This affection of siding with the ignorant may be an effective wile on the part of a smart controversialist, anxious more for popular support than for truth, but it will not deceive those who have felt concerned to understand these matters . . . one finds a most important difference between the principles of the ordinary and the naturalistic schools. The one finds its admiration for representations of nature excited by the truth with which the subtleties of a beautiful scene are rendered, the other lays greater stress on the decorative cleverness with which the space devoted to the picture is filled by lines and masses. The one finds its poetry in the scene, the other claims that it is added from without. The one must work under the inspiration of the subject, the other can grind out its combinations according to rule in the studio, because it is not nature, it is so-called art that is wanted, as though art were past pictures and not capable of change and development in its principles.
>
> . . . Mr Robinson is consumed by a fear that his opponents will never be satisfied. The question naturally arises, satisfied with what? With his defence of outrageous combination landscape painting? There has been no defence. With his justification of the use of lady models as rustics? Not a soul thinks of imitating him.
>
> . . . If it is one of Mr Robinson's pleasantries to persistently write the word naturalistic as opposed to artistic, perhaps it ought to be pointed out that the opposite of naturalism is artificialism, a point worth thinking upon my friend.[14]

The furore caused by Emerson was obviously not one which was going to fade away. *Naturalistic Photography*, acting as a catalyst, had created a revolution within photographic circles, bringing together those who demanded more from the photographic image than the seemingly facile and theatrical productions currently in vogue would allow them.

The publication of the book had divided leading photographers into two camps, and the fight for supremacy began in earnest. Sad to say, many would-be naturalistic photographers misunderstood or ignored the finer points of Emerson's text. In his own hands 'naturalistic' focusing was used sensitively in an unobtrusive manner, but the 'fuzzy' pictures that Emerson had warned against began to proliferate and where he had approached his subjects in as unsentimental and straightforward a manner as his Victorian attitudes would allow, many of his adherents merely copied the formal qualities that made 'naturalistic' photographs so visually strong. Soon many who opposed his views simply thought of him as the man who photographed everything out of focus. For example, Andrew Pringle writing in *The Studio* of 1893 in an article entitled 'The Naissance of Art in Photography' says:

> The crusade against superfluous detail led to many follies and extravagances. For a time we had quite a run on very rough papers for prints, even of the smallest sizes. The prints were simply smudges in most cases; true texture was lost. We ran riot in fuzziness. Pictures were, and are, made so much out of focus that the outlines are doubled, and spotty 'areas of confusion' are seen with an effect almost sickening. One set of evils is eliminated at the expense of another set no less objectionable; but it is to be hoped that in time we may return to moderation. Many have accepted the example of Dr Emerson without rushing into extremes. . . .'

However, Emerson's unshakable belief in his own philosophy was sufficient to continue his missionary zeal. In 1890 he presented a copy of *Pictures of East Anglian Life* to each of the photographic societies in England – *Naturalistic Photography* had been unillustrated, and, wrote Emerson, 'I have been led to take this step from a sense of duty to the earnest student, for my views have been misrepresented . . . that the student ought to have some tangible results to study.'[15]

However, Emerson's detractors continued to bludgeon him on every possible opportunity – later that year at the Photographic Convention held in July, Philip Newman, an artist who disliked the naturalistic school of painting, delivered a lecture 'Imagining and Imaging' – a stinging attack on Emerson's proposition that reality could ever be better than that which was created out of the artist's own mind and imagination. Reality, argued Newman, could never match the perfection that exists within the soul of 'true artists'. True to form, Emerson issued an equally stinging reply, condemning Newman as a 'third rate decorative painter' and saying 'The naturalists are justified, and as every cause gains by futile attacks, so shall we grow stronger from the incapacity of our enemies.'[16]

By 1891, the almost continual arguing seemed to have become commonplace. The shock waves of *Naturalistic Photography* had died down. But Emerson, a man of considerable principle, was not content to rest on his laurels. Since the publication of his book he had continued to research and advance his ideas; ever attempting to extend his theories, he investigated art and science – working towards the day when art and photography would become united and photography could stand alone.

Oddly Emerson's photographs did not support his theories as one would expect. According to him they were first and foremost art photographs, but the scientist in him seemed to over-shadow the would-be artist. His end products were not, as were Robinson's, individual images, each one isolated from the next. Although his photographs were frequently to be found hung on exhibition walls, his real outlet was in the form of books and portfolios. These consisted of a series of images backed by descriptive texts.

The information was collected entirely through his own observations. The subject matter of all these is the lifestyle and customs of the Norfolk and Suffolk broadland dwellers, and collectively they make a sensitive and important document. His strongest images tend to be those of the reed-cutters and eel-catchers in their boats, amid the wide expanse of still water and flat landscape. It is here that the strange, remote and placid atmosphere comes over with a force quite absent in the work of his rivals.

It was characteristic of Emerson to devote much time to experiencing first-hand the life of the people he was recording. He would rise early to explore the rivers, creeks and broads. As he roamed the desolate landscape he would absorb all he came across, always making a written description, but not always photographing. He was, one morning, astonished to encounter an enormous congregation of fishermen arranged on the bank between two tall poles driven into the river bottom. At the striking of a large dinner gong there began immediate and intensive fishing. After a pre-determined time the gong was again struck, at which signal fishing ceased. Emerson soon discovered that this was a fishing competition arranged by one of the local publicans. The general purpose became obvious when most of the prize money melted quickly into beer and whisky in his own establishment.

It says a great deal for Emerson's personality and skill that he succeeded in penetrating the exceedingly efficient underground protection system of some of the Norfolk poachers. On numerous occasions he would set out with a couple of men at dusk. A word in the ear of a local road worker might reveal information about any areas being watched that night, and they would spend the night netting pheasants and partridges in reasonable safety. As dawn approached they would return to a little cottage in a desolate spot on the marshes where they could leave the bag, now containing some seventy or eighty birds and hares. The woman of the house produced breakfast of beer and cheese, and eventually they would leave unhurriedly at first light. She would arrange the sale of the booty, often to rich buyers as far away as London, and one of the men usually returned some days later to collect the money. In this way they made reasonable, though dangerous, living.

It was typical of Emerson's depth of involvement that he was deeply concerned about the social imbalances that drove people to poaching: Norfolk was, in those days, a grossly polarised and feudal community, with very rich landowners and extremely badly paid farm labourers, who were forced to exist under appalling living conditions. They thus turned to alternative means. The utmost caution and an underground communica-tion network was necessary because the penalties, at that time were very heavy and Emerson pointed out that the juries who imposed such crippling fines, or jail sentences, very often comprised the landowners themselves whose land was being poached. This obviously made fair trials a farce, and he proceeded to play an active part in the uphill fight to rectify the situation.

Herein lies the paradox of Emerson; according to his own statement at the time he set out to produce pictures whose purpose was to give aesthetic pleasure – documentary is a term never once mentioned, let alone discussed. Yet his photographs are undoubtedly documentary. He could almost be construed as the first 'concerned photographer'. His verbose discourses on photography as art appear inconsistent with the impression of genuine sympathy with the environment he photographed created in his books. What makes Emerson so difficult to comprehend is that he was confused by his own diversity.

One of the most memorable of his exertions must have been his weeks spent living on his friend Thomas Goodall's houseboat, when, together, they made *Wild Life on a Tidal Water*. By day they both worked, Emerson photographing, Goodall painting in his studio on board. By night they would write, talk, drink port and smoke. Their sailor, Joey, 'a wild-looking East Anglian, with long lank hair flowing over his sun-burnt face', would venture abroad to consume large quantities of ale before returning to cook the evening meal. We know very little of Goodall's work, but the one painting reproduced here suggests that he worked closely with Emerson, in this case obviously painting directly from the photograph, altering only the background and perspective.

Bow Net (1886) by T. F. Goodall. Emerson's artistic companion and collaborator on several projects remains something of a mystery and his work is still almost completely unknown. Compare this painting with Plate 29. Oil on canvas, 33 × 50 inches. Walker Art Gallery, Liverpool. Photograph courtesy of the Witt Library, Courtauld Institute, University of London.

Emerson's works were always beautifully produced, usually in large format, their splendour enhanced by the fact that they were often put out in limited editions. He took pains to record the numbers sold, and often the names of those who bought them. When an edition expired all the plates were destroyed.

But outside the production of his photographs, Emerson's love for the political arena continued and in December 1890 he announced to a surprised public that 'the limitations of photography are so great that, though the results may and sometimes do give a certain aesthetic pleasure, the medium must always rank the lowest of the arts.' Much to the incredulity of his followers, he had decided to recant! A great painter whom he refused to name, but was probably his friend James McNeil Whistler, had convinced him that photography was not an art. Also a careful study of Hurter and Driffield's pioneering work in the field of sensitometry had led him to deduce that it was not possible to exert sufficient control over plate and print development to achieve the interpretation of nature central to his philosophy.* In a brave gesture typical of his earlier pronunciations, Emerson had privately printed a black-bordered pamphlet – *The Death of Naturalistic Photography* – in which he explained:

'The individuality of the artist is cramped – control of the picture is possible to a *slight* degree by varied focusing by varying the exposure but this is working in the dark, by development I doubt . . . and lastly, by a certain choice in printing methods. But the all-vital powers of selection and rejection are totally limited, bound in by fixed and narrow barriers. No differential analysis can be made, no subduing of parts, save by dodging – no emphasis – save by dodging, and that is not pure photography, impure photography is merely a confession of limitations.

'I thought once (Hurter and Driffield have taught me differently) that true values could be *altered at will* by development. They therefore talk of getting values . . . true to nature is to talk nonsense.

'. . . I have, I regret it deeply, compared photographs to great works of

*Photographers familiar with Ansel Adams' zone system will recognise the fallacies in this argument.

art and photographers to great artists. It was rash and thoughtless and my punishment is having to acknowledge it now.

'. . . In short, I throw my lot in with those who say that Photography is a very limited art. I deeply regret that I have come to this conclusion.'
Whether art or not, Emerson's followers were not to be so easily turned against photography and neither, it would appear, was Emerson. His confession of failure as intense and pedantic as had been his earlier works did not prevent him from continuing to produce pictures though after the dramatic *Death of Naturalistic Photography* his active participation in the politics of the medium declined.

However, his reputation survived. Eight years after, in 1899 a third edition of *Naturalistic Photography* appeared with a revised final chapter explaining the fallacy of photography as art. In the same year a dinner in Emerson's honour was organised by a group of friends and admirers. At the request of the guests he was asked to comment on the progress of photography over the past ten years. Emerson explained that he had with much interest followed the course of picture-taking through the pages of *Photograms of the Year* (an annual visual digest of photography) and exhibition catalogues, and had reached the regretful conclusion that pictorial photography was on the down grade:

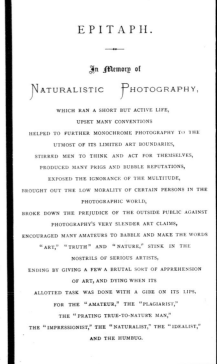

A page from *The Death of Naturalistic Photography*. Courtesy of the Royal Photographic Society.

> Ten years ago there were a few men who had begun to see the possibilities of photography and who were exploring legitimate fields in which it could not be rivalled by any other means of artistic expression. Now these men seemed to have retired or to have been overwhelmed by a wave of imitation of other arts and of efforts for bold meretricious 'effects'. Some of the lauded leaders were insincere: other surreptitiously copying the themes and methods of third rate but popular painters.[17]

With a spirit reminiscent of his fiery invective of a decade earlier, he went on to tell the diners that the only thing to awaken photography from its illusions would be an unflinching attack upon, and exposure of, some of those men who have been looked upon as leaders!

Curiously, it would seem that his continued interest in photography was the public sign of a certain lack of faith in his condemnation of the artistic possibilities of the medium. All the available evidence would suggest that it was the painter Whistler who had made Emerson announce 'the death of Naturalistic Photography' and yet as late as 1893 the two were still corresponding on the subject. In May of that year Whistler wrote to Emerson from Paris, thanking him for some photographs and saying 'how very kind and nice of you to send me those most curiously attractive photographs. I should more simply say pictures, for they certainly are pictures, and very fine ones!'

But despite this apparent renewal of interest Emerson's involvement seems to have grown increasingly academic. In 1892 he credited himself with having produced the first ever portrait taken with a telephoto lens, while in 1914 he records having produced both a stereoscopic slide 'to show how the stereoscope renders delicate atmospheric effects' and an autochrome colour picture – 'Portrait of a Lady.'[18]

However, Emerson's revival of enthusiasm was not restricted to writing and in 1925, he embarked on a new photographic venture. Typical of his vanity and flair for the dramatic, he commissioned J. Harvard Thomas, a sculptor, to produce silver and bronze medallions to be presented to photographers for 'artistic' merit – the obverse bearing the Emerson profile. The 'Emerson' medals were awarded over a period of seven years, silvers going to those Emerson considered particularly innovative and true to photographic art while the bronze went to those he felt to be worthy but less distinguished. Curiously, together with his returning interest in photography, Emerson appeared to have revised his opinions on the worth of certain photographers. To Julie Lourberg, a Dane, went a silver medal 'for studio portraits' – Julia Margaret Cameron, who had received much praise in earlier years was only awarded a bronze. In all, he gave fifty-seven medals, the final going to Brassai in 1933 for his book *Paris le Nuit*. Emerson's awards seemed popular and shortly after he instituted a new scheme, giving bronze medals to 'any deserving print'.*

Beyond this he appears not to have pursued photography with any great vigour until 1924 when he began work on *A History of Art Photography* and a fourth edition of *Naturalistic Photography*. Neither were published.

Emerson died in 1936 on the eve of his eightieth birthday and is buried in Falmouth. Despite the relatively short duration of his concern for photography and despite his attempts to stop the activity he had set in motion, by starting the first revolution in photography, he has left a strong tradition of image making that exists still today, a tradition of an honest and unsentimentalised recording of what is revealed as a fine art through the sensitivity of the photographer.

For all his sincerity, Emerson was both dogmatic and, apparently, confused. The main stream of his thinking was simple and direct: to establish photography as an independent art form by stressing the qualities that make it unique. Unfortunately, to achieve this end, Emerson rather lost himself in attempting to establish a relationship between Art, Nature and Science and in a wilderness of half-understood art history. It is ironic that in making his major thesis, that photography had gone astray by attempting to imitate painting, Emerson advocated a similar course of action himself – simply rejecting one mode of painting in favour of another. However, through this confusion his clear thinking on photograph's singular strength appears time and time again. It is this influence on the medium that is of importance, and for this that P. H. Emerson should be remembered.

*A complete list of medallists is to be found in the Appendix.

Emerson's Technique

Emerson experimented with and investigated a wide range of techniques and equipment and, as one might expect, arrived at a straightforward and standardised system.

He normally used a half or whole plate, or sometimes a 10×8-inch camera. Speed of action was of no consequence to him and he decried the use of small hand-held cameras, whose quality left much to be desired. Because of the difficult geographical conditions under which he usually worked, humping about anything much bigger than a 10×8-inch camera presented considerable problems. Occasionally, however, he used an enormous 22×24-inch camera, chiefly for large exhibition prints. He cites one traumatic escapade when he had to enlist the aid of two peasants to move such a camera, all set up with tripod, from one Norfolk marsh to another. He inevitably worked with a tripod, or some other means of stabilisation. He frequently operated from a small boat, and would sometimes clamp the camera to the gunwale, or alternatively lash eight-foot poles to each leg of the tripod and set up directly in the water. It is as well that the waterways of East Anglia are shallow, for the winds are fast, and Emerson and his outfit were by no means stable; disaster nearly ensued on numerous occasions.

He used Dallmeyer's long-focus landscape lens, in two or three focal lengths. This he discovered in 1888 and found the best for his purpose because, at full aperture it gave an image of soft outline and minimal distortion. He chose focal lengths on the long side because he considered that they produced a more natural rendering of perspective.

His dry-plates were then developed as soon as possible, certainly on the same day, 'while the impression was still fresh'. He found that gelatino-bromide plates gave truer tonal relationships than wet-plates, as well as being faster, thus affording him shorter exposure times.

Most of all Emerson was involved in the finished print and methods for its reproduction. For printing he quickly arrived at the platinum process as ideal for achieving the results he was after. The image was soft with delicate tonal gradations and an absence of total black, a phenomenon, he thought, non-existent in nature. So obsessed did he become with the platinotye that he stated: 'If the photoetching process and the platinotype process were to become lost arts, we, for our part, should never take another photograph.' It also had the advantage of being more permanent than silver prints. Because his output was chiefly in the form of books and portfolios it was absolutely crucial to find a reproduction method which preserved the quality and feeling of the original print as closely as possible.

With painstaking thoroughness he approached thirteen different firms who practised photo-etching, gave them all negatives without issuing any specific instructions, and was dismayed by the results. They were all grossly retouched. He finally found two men, Mr Dawson and Mr Colls, who between them were using a photogravure process which required no retouching. These two were connected with the Typographical Etching Company and the Autotype Company, both of London. Their autogravure process was usually used where Emerson's books employed photo-mechanical reproduction. Because the images were taken from his negatives, not prints, and made under his scrutinous direction they were, to all intents and purposes, original prints. (In some of his smaller limited editions he would actually use platinum prints – one can imagine the time and extraordinary effort involved.) It is worth describing, in Coll's words this technique, since it was of such great importance to Emerson.

A polished copper-plate, preferably a hammered one, is thoroughly cleaned, to remove all traces of grease, and is dusted over with powdered asphalt or resin, and the plate heated until the powder becomes partially melted. A carbon print from a reversed transparency is next developed upon the grained plate and allowed to dry. The unprotected margin is then painted round with asphalt, or other resist-varnish, and a wall of bordering wax placed round the work. It is then ready for biting, which is done with perchloride of iron, the bare portions being first attacked; water is then added, and the biting proceeds to the next tone, and so on, adding water when required, until the solution has penetrated the thickest portions of the film. The greatest care must be exercised during this operation, and a careful watch kept lest the action remain too long on any part. The biting should proceed in a gradual manner, so that the values are not exaggerated. The plate is then rinsed in water, the bordering wax removed, and the pigment cleaned off with a little potash ley.[19]

About 3,000 impressions could be pulled from these plates.

Emerson's efforts were justified; the quality of the autogravures though subtley different from that of his platinum prints, is equally beautiful and in no way inferior.

Emerson did not enlarge his plates, so all his original prints were made as 'contacts'. He condemned enlarging as not only detracting from quality, but also realised that there was no relation between size and artistic value. They were all undoctored with the exception of clouds. He considered it permissible to 'burn-in' clouds, or print them from another negative, so long as this represented a closer approach to the feeling of the natural situation.

Plates

[4]

P.H.EMERSON. [13]

P. H. EMERSON

P.H.EMERSON.

P.H.EMERSON. [38]

P.H.Emerson.

P.H.EMERSON

P.H.EMERSON

P. H. EMERSON

P.H. Emerson

P.H.EMERSON.

[57]

[59]

P.H.EMERSON.

[61]

form so prominent and picturesque a feature in the landscape. The dense green masses of this plant, so characteristic of the Broads in the summer time, after putting forth their purple flower tassles, and undergoing the most beautiful changes of subtle and delicate colour in the autumn, shed their leaves, and by Christmas nothing remains but the tall, slender, sapless stems with the withered flowers at the tips.

The cutting and harvesting of the reed afford profitable employment to the Broadman, marshman, or farm-hand during the winter months, when other work is scarce; and whenever the weather permits they may be seen busily plying the meak amid the tall yellow masses, or bringing the loaded marsh-boat across the Broad. Each of these four plates [nos. 8, 9, 10 and 11] portrays some characteristic incident of this picturesque labour. First is the single figure of a reed-cutter at work. Standing with his crotch-boots in the water, he bends over in the act of cutting a fresh shoof, those just cut lying behind him bound with a band of a few crossed and twisted reeds.

Being a piece-worker, the reed-cutter is his own master, and consequently the work is much in demand by those men – often some of the best hands – who like, occasionally, to relieve the monotony of existence by a prolonged drinking-bout, or to whom the attractions of a coursing meeting on the marshes, or a shooting match, are irresistible. When cut, the shooves are stood on end, leaning against each other in stacks on the bank of the nearest dyke, till the marsh-boat conveys them to the staithe, where they are ricked.

Plate 9: *Towing the Reed* (LLNB XXVI)
Towing the Reed illustrates the usual method of getting the loaded boat along the narrow water-arteries which intersect the marshes, and afford communication with the reed-beds. Sturdy of frame and strong-featured, a fine type of the Norfolk peasant is this tower.

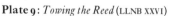

Plate 10: *Ricking the Reed* (LLNB XXVII)
Then we have the men at the rick on the staithe, at the head of a long dyke stretching far away to the distance.

Plate 11: *During the Reed Harvest* (LLNB XXVIII)
And again a gang of workers forming a busy scene in the heart of the reed grounds.

Plate 12: *Snipe-Shooting* (LLNB X)
Snipe-shooting forms the subject of our present picture. Three men with guns and dogs are wading across a bit of marsh skirting the Broad, followed on the dyke wall by a boy who carries the few birds, including a wild duck, which have already fallen. The water is a little too high to-day for good sport, but now and again, from some little tufty island, a snipe will rise with sharp startled cry, and that odd jerky flight so trying to the skill of the gunner. A teal or mallard, too, will be walked up, and the dogs will certainly hunt out some water-hens from their hiding-places. Some sportsman may object to the breed of the dog in the foreground. Well, in spite of his looks, he will fetch duck or snipe in a style which might make any professed retriever jealous. He, like his master, is taking a day's holiday from the more serious duties of the farm. Minding stock is his business, sport his pleasure. He is a most intelligent sample of canine accomplishment. We have seen him course, turn, and kill a hare in one field in the cleverest manner. He delights to follow the gun, and well repays his master for the care bestowed on his education.

Plate 13: *At the Covert Corner* (PEAL XI)
The sun rises higher, and the frosty feather-tracery melts; still the keeper strides on, now and then adding to his bag. Over marsh, and along river-walls, and through old reed-beds has he sped, and now at noon we find him in the alder carrs near home. Here he has been sorting his bag, and deciding what he will do with the birds, how he will take his master the snipe, how he will eat the mallard himself, and how he will give the owl to the village doctor, who is a bird-collector. In the midst of his calculations, however, he decides to have a pipe, and with some difficulty lights it, for the wind is strong as well as keen, and bends the reed ere it reaches him. After he has lighted his pipe, he will tie up his birds in separate lots and replace them in the bag, then he will go up the road to his cottage ready for his dinner.

Plate 14: *Gunner Working up to Fowl* (LLNB XIX)
No boat is handier, or more perfectly adapted to its special purpose, than the gun-punt. The draught of water being only a few inches, the shallowest places are easily accessible to it. The bottom is flat from side to side, but curved slightly from stem to stern, like the line of a skate-blade. The sides, which converge to a point at either end, are flat, and slope outwards at a slight angle – the floor of the boat being of less area than the top. As may be seen in the pictures, [nos. 14 and 15] the centre only of the boat is open, the ends being covered with a gently-sloping deck. A first-class gun-punt has very subtle lines, and can only be built properly

by the most intelligent of boat-wrights, and perhaps only by one who is himself a gunner. The punt can be sailed, rowed, quanted, or sculled, is light and fast, while its exceedingly low freeboard offers a minimum of resistance to wind and wave when the weather is boisterous. Under the decked ends are stowed the ammunition, the shoulder-guns, the oiled coat and sou'-wester, the snack of food and drop of rum, and other needs or comforts of the gunner.

The big gun is nicely poised on a swivel, the stout iron pin of which works in a socket drilled into a massive block of hard wood, which, according to the size of the weapon, is either fixed or allowed to slide in a short run on the bottom of the boat, the recoil being checked by a powerful spring. Boat and gun are painted a leaden grey, or, as the men will tell you, 'the colour of the water,' invisibility being the most desired attribute of the wild-fowler.

In our first picture a gunner, in the grey morning light, which the tone of the plate so well renders, is sculling up to some fowl which he has marked down among the rushes in a shallow corner of the Broad. Lying right down in the bottom of his punt, no part of him can be seen from the water, save the hand which grasps the short straight-bladed oar with which he sculls. Like all the gunners, he is wonderfully adept in this method of propulsion – working up to the birds swiftly and noiselessly, and steering with great facility. From his prone position he is just able to see his course, and train the gun, without alarming the wild-ducks. Possibly the end-on view of the punt and gun looks to them like a strange bird on the water, and excites merely curiosity or wonder. At times, during the winter, large numbers of foreign fowl come over, and, if the Broads are frozen, they will light on the ice, or in the wake which the Broadman breaks, and keeps open as long as possible, in order to attract them. Then the gunner pulls his punt on to the ice, and shoving it along with a short iron-pointed stick, works up to within shooting distance.

Plate 15: *The Fowler's Return* (LLNB XX)
Our fowler is returning to the boat-shelter where he houses his punt. Another sportsman has come to have a look at the few birds he has bagged, and to compare notes as to the events of the morning.

Plate 16: *Water-Lilies* (LLNB VIII)
The beautiful perennial aquatic herbs of the poetically-named order *Nymphæaceæ* are common throughout the Broads. They were so called, perhaps because, like the nymphs, they delighted in sequestered pools and shady streams. The two children of the family common in this country are the *Nuphar*, or yellow water-lily, and the *Nymphæa*, or white water-lily. The yellow lily is locally called

'brandy-bottle', on account of the alcoholic odour given off by the blossoms. This plant is far less pretentious in its beauty than the white water-lily, though the habits of the two are much alike, save that the latter hides its fruit under water until it is ripe.

Plate 17: *Gathering Water-Lilies* (LLNB IX)

Plate 18: *Blackshore* (River Blythe, Suffolk) (PEAL XVI)
A few cottages clustering round a small tavern, 'The Fishing-Buss', whose name bespeaks its history, a cow-house, a quay in places decayed, a couple of condemned smacks' hulls lying alongside the quay or drawn up on the land, and occasionally a weather-worn 'billy-boy' moored to the quay – this is Blackshore on the River Blythe – Blackshore, of which we read that once spacious warehouses were erected on its wharf 'for the stowage of nets and other stores, one room of which is capable of holding a thousand tons of salt'; that a dock was made there in 1783, and that in the same year twenty fishing-busses met there for the white-herring fishery. It seems this quay was made in James the First's reign, and must have been the scene of busy life when Dunwich, Walberswick, and Southwold were flourishing with their fisheries; but as the greater places fell to nothingness, so has this little place proportionately fallen into utter decay, though perhaps we are not strictly correct in this statement, for the last time we saw Blackshore it was again in the hands of the builder – two cottages were being run up.

Our plate shows the hamlet as seen from the cansey leading to the ferry between Southwold and Walberswick, and in the picture can be seen the newly-made horse-ferry, standing where it was left for weeks before it was launched in the muddy Blythe. Some sheep are feeding along the cansey, as is their wont in early spring, the shepherd following them. At the old decayed quay is moored the schooner 'Heart of Oak,' well known to Southwold and Walberswick fishermen, for in her more than one of them have sailed along the coast, and some we know have nearly met their deaths on her; but the sturdy vessel survived, and now she floats at Blackshore quay condemned as unseaworthy. Close by is a creek called Buss Creek, because an old Dutch buss was dug up there many years ago. The adventurous Dutchmen, it is said, used to arrive at Blackshore with herrings before the English herring-fisheries were established; here they delivered their herrings, and then fished for sparling (smelts).

Plate 19: *Cantley: Wherries Waiting for the Turn of the Tide* (LLNB XXIV)

One can hardly imagine the Broads without wherries. They are to be seen moored at every staithe, as well as in the most sequestered bights, often giving no sign of life save that of the galley fire, whose smoke curls lazily upwards. If it be summer time, the skipper's family, dog and all, will be seen on deck from morn till night. At nearly every bend of the river the brown mainsail, filled by the breeze, will quickly carry the curious craft out of your sight, whilst you are wondering whence appeared this picturesque barge, and whither it is bound.

These vessels are built of oak, with the exception of the masts and gaff, which are made of American fir. Their average register is twenty-five tons. A portion is separated from the hold at the stern, and fitted with seats and lockers, a stove being placed amidships. The cost of building a wherry is about £7 a ton, exclusive of sail and mast. The rig is a mainsail rig, the sail and gaff being raised by one rope by means of a windlass; and so heavy are these that it is considered quite a feat for a man to raise the sail completely without stopping. This is often a matter for modest bets. Two are required for a crew, and although at times one man can manage, they always 'look to have two men', as they say. These men are paid by the voyage, an average wage being thirty shillings from Norwich to Yarmouth; and since they are paid by the voyage, it is evident they will strain every nerve to make quick passages. More rarely the men in the large wherries are paid by freight; then the two men get sevenpence in every shilling and the owner of the wherry fivepence. They have bills of lading just like merchantmen. Some firms have tried to introduce steam wherries, and on the Yare they are successful, but not on the Bure or Thurne, for on these latter rivers weeds are so common that the propellers get clogged.

The railways have taken away much of the work of the wherries, but there is still a great number employed on the different rivers. Lately a good many pleasure wherries have been built. They are very comfortable, and are the best boats for cruising on the Broads, as they only draw from two to three feet of water, and sailing as they do very close to the wind, they are most handy for navigating the district. The hire of one of these, with the crew of two men, costs from £8 to £10 a week.

Fifty years ago a twelve-tonner was considered a large-sized wherry. The rule of the road in sailing is that those who have a fair wind give way to the others. No mast lights are used, and it is said no claim can be made for any accident after nine o'clock at night. They pay tonnage for landing a cargo at a staithe, and in Yarmouth they have to pay harbour dues. The chief cargoes are coal, sugar, oilcake, groceries, several kinds of manure, horns and bones, and timber.

The quant is a most important implement in wherry navigation. It is a fir pole twenty-four feet long, with an elm shoulder and cap. The shoulder is put on the bottom, and the wherry-man then places the cap or head against his shoulder and walks along the narrow counter the whole length of the wherry, throwing his weight the whole time on to the quant. On arriving at the end he cleverly and easily lifts the quant out of the water, walks back, replants it, and repeats the operation. The quant is used when wind or tide are unfavourable. Forby says the word quant is derived from the Latin *contus*, a pole. The wherrymen are a fine set of men, and require all their strength for their work. It is a regular occupation, and the men, jealous of outsiders, do not care to take any crew not brought up to the work from boyhood. They are very respectable, drink little, and have a wondrous fellow-feeling for each other. They carry very little beer with them, but drink cold tea to quench their thirst. When they arrive at a waterside tavern, however, they assemble in the taproom and enjoy their beer. This is usually when there is a 'shoulder-breeze' on – or, in other words, when wind and tide are unfavourable, and they must use the quant. They are sportsmen in their own way, and can be seen at times eel-picking as they sail along, or trolling for pike. In the evening, when at rest, they fish for eels or bream. In winter they carry a gun, and, with their dog, manage to provide themselves with plover and other wild-fowl. Our second plate shows two wherries waiting at Cantley for the turn of the tide. This is a famous half-way house, and often in summer one will see them thickly congregated round the staithe.

Plate 20: *A Reed Boat-House* (LLNB XXXI)

A common sight on the Broads is the boat-house, now standing exposed on the river bank, now peeping from a mass of rush, now sheltered in a clump of trees. But few of these are beautiful; their hard lines and symmetrical reed thatch offend the eye. Not so, however, with this little structure, which we discovered one wintry afternoon. The sun was passing behind a cloud as we first came upon this picture, and the lighting was beautifully soft and subdued, as it fell upon the reed walls and thatched roof, throwing at the same time a reflection of the most tender delicacy and grace. In the foreground were some withered stalks, reminding one of poor Bonvin's fine feeling and delicate drawing; behind lay the softened background of the Broad, and on the right grew two trees – the wispy trees beloved of Corot. There is little in this gem but fine quality and the charm and fascination of tranquil repose in atmosphere and water, teaching that simplicity and senti- ment are at the foundation of all true art.

Plate 21: *A Norfolk Boat-Yard* (LLNB XIII)
Here, at the boat-yard, a boat-wright and his man are busily at work dressing with tar a flat- bottomed reed-boat, making it all tight and ready for the winter's work. The man tends the fire and stirs the boiling tar, while, half hidden by the misty smoke which drives across the picture, the master vigorously applies his long- handled brush to the weak places on the vessel. Around are other boats and the varied lumber inseparable from a boat-yard.

Plate 22: *Poling the Marsh Hay* (LLNB XVII)
Long after haysel is over on the uplands the marshmen are busily engaged, under the broiling sun of July and August, cutting and carrying, by land or water, the heavy green crops from the marsh land. The more cultivated and thoroughly-drained marshes yield a hay of high quality, while the rough stuff which grows in abundance on the half-drained ground, or on the rands and walls of the river, though too coarse for fodder, makes valuable litter. Splen- did the mowers look, as they sweep down the tall rank herbage; their loose shirts, of white or blue cotton, with sleeves turned back to the elbow, gleam in the sunshine; their legs are encased in the tall marsh boots, without which they could not work in comfort on the swampy soil. Strapped to their backs are their hones; wide, soft felt hats cover their heads, pictur- esquely shadowing their faces. Superb is the action of the men as they bend to the heavy work, or, standing with booted legs wide apart, hone their scythes, or wipe the gathered moisture from their faces.

For an hour before and after noon they rest from their labour. Forming a social group in the shade of the alder bushes, each one eats the 'bit of wittles' brought to him along the marsh wall by wife or daughter, now and again taking a long drink of cold tea, or home-brewed from the bottle. The meal over, some doze, others angle in the river, till the two resting hours have sped.

When dry, the hay is forked up into heaps: these are borne to the nearest dyke on two poles, passed underneath in such a manner as to support the load when carried by two men walking between them, one in front of and one behind the burden. This picturesque mode of conveyance is adopted because the load has to be carried over ground so soft that cart or barrow would be worse than useless. At the dyke the hay is pitched into large flat-bottomed boats, and rowed or quanted away to some staithe, where it is piled on shore ready for the waggons which bear it away to the farmyard.

In sharp contrast to this bright July idyl is the sombre grey tone of *Poling the Marsh Hay*

– quite as beautiful, but much sadder in its sentiment. On a dull November day some poor peasants are bringing home the remnants of their crop, which, left too late, has been caught by the autumnal floods, and lain for weeks soaking in the water. When the water fell the sodden heaps were moved, and placed on the marsh wall to dry, and they are now poling them away to the litter-stack. On those marshes which are not protected from the tides by walls, the crop is frequently ruined by the rising of the waters. Often, just when it is ready to carry, a north-west wind, acting on a spring tide, will force up the water in a day and night, to remain at flood-level for weeks together. At times, over many acres of marshes, sheets of water may be seen dotted all over by the round tops of the soaking cocks of litter, which too often rot and spoil before the floods subside.

Plate 23: *The Fringe of the Marsh* (LLNB XXXIX)
In *The Fringe of the Marsh* much interesting and paintable material comes very happily together. Variety is added by a patch of gorse to a soft grassy foreground, already broken by the water, which takes the eye into the picture by two ways – one straight up the dyke under the dark hawthorns, the other gracefully curving. Against the sky the beautiful silhouette of the group of cottages tells sharply, in pleasing contrast to the softer outlines of the trees. The light just catches the roadway winding past the houses to where the distant marshes form a straight horizon, broken only by a few wisps of trees.

Plate 24: *The Old Order and the New* (LLNB XII)
One lovely summer's evening we moored our boat by burying our rond-anchor in a bank of springy turf, covered with tufts of delicately- scented spirea, sedge and fern, from which the setting sun cast long shadows. Far as eye could reach wandered the silver stream. On either hand stretched low marshes – some cultivated and dotted with the white shirts of mowers who had borne the heat and burden of the day; others richly coloured with grass and patches of red and white cattle, who by their whisking tails and tossing heads drove off the flies. A wherry with brown mainsail and gaily-painted hull sailed down the river, brushing the sweet- sedge and yellow-iris on the bank. The breeze was laden with the scent of hay-field and bean- field, mingled with rare puffs of the exquisite perfume of sweet-gale. The flowering rush, the white-petalled arrow-head, and the water-lily gave brightness to the picture. To the westward the sky turned to a golden orange, slashed with bars of grey. The effect on the landscape was magical; trees, windmills, farmsteads were bathed in a golden light, which softened their contours and gave them unwonted splendour.

Plate 25: *A Suffolk Dyke* (PLFF IX)

Plate 29: *Setting the Bow-Net* (LLNB II)
Here we have an old Broadman and his daughter out in their flat-bottomed boat on a hot July afternoon, about to drop a bow-net into a likely corner of the Broad to catch some tench, that most edible of fish, firm and glutinous – the sole of the fresh waters.

The net, deftly braided by the girl's skilled fingers, has been bent by the old man to hoops of split hazel, and set taut by sticks of the same, notched at either end to fit the outer hoops, thus holding them wide apart, and forming a firm cylindrical cage. From each end springs a cone-shaped inner net which, tapering to the centre of the cage, has an opening at its apex; these openings are the entrances to the trap; a string fastened to the hoop at the opposite end holds each one in position. A very large fish can easily push its way into these openings, but a small one would have much difficulty in getting out again, even if it managed to find the hole. The old man is putting a stone in the net to keep it on the bottom.

are as well marked as a rabbit run. The nets, when not in use, are generally kept fastened upon hoops, and, when required, are 'set up' by stiffening the hoops by means of sticks, as shown in the plate. These two old fellows, one an octogenarian and the other nearly so, have stood the seasons' changes well, and are as case-hardened as the old bow-net itself. They were kindly, obliging souls, as we have ever found these Norfolk peasants, not wishing to know if we were going to 'sell their picture in Lunnon', never misusing an 'h', quiet, witty, dignified, and free from all vulgarity.

Plate 26: *Rowing Home the Schoof-Stuff* (LLNB XXI)
The word 'schoof' or 'schoaf' is derived from the Dutch *schoof*, and originally meant a sheaf of wheat: from this it came to mean, in Norfolk at least, a sheaf of anything, for there we constantly hear of schooves of gladdon, schooves of reed. Schoof-stuff, however, has a distinct meaning of its own, and is used to describe the crop of marsh-plants which, too rough for fodder and too mixed for thatching, are yet cut to be used for covering beet, for stable litter, and finally for manure. The chief plants comprehended under the name schoof-stuff are the bolder, yellow-iris, inferior gladdon, bur rush, sweet rush, common rush, sword grass, *carices*, rush grasses, bents, fecuses, hair grasses, cotton grasses, and others which thrive in marshes and lands periodically flooded. Of all these plants, says one authority on agriculture, cattle will only eat two or three kinds of *juncus*, while another admits having seen them crop a species of carex. Schoof-stuff is surely, then, not ill named.

This old Broadman has been along the Broad edge, cutting his schoof-stuff, and is now rowing it home to his cottage, where he will dry it and store it. He has cut a great deal more than he will require for his own use, so he will sell some of it to a neighbouring farmer for 'kivering beet'.

Plate 30: *The Eel-Catcher's Home* (LLNB VI)
Familiar to all frequenters of the Broads are the quaint, ark-like house-boats of the eel-catchers. Here we have one of these cosy habitations, built on the hull of some old smack's boat, squeezed perhaps in the rough work of ferrying fish to the steamer which carries the catch of the North Sea Fleet to the London market, condemned and sold for a few shillings to its present owner.

Plate 27: *Marsh Man Going to Cut Schoof-Stuff* (LLNB XXII)
The young marshman in the second plate has shouldered his meak, and now the gladdon is cut and the reed not yet ripe, he will fill up his time before the flighting hour in getting a boat-load of schoof-stuff for his grandfather's and his own cow-house, which stand near together behind the rick.

Plate 31: *Taking Up the Eel-Net* (LLNB VII)
As soon as the temperature of the water rises with the warmth of spring, in April or early May, the eels leave the mud and begin to move. The pick now gives place to hook and line. Procuring small roach with a cast-net or hand-net such as the man is using in our picture, he baits his lines and liggers, putting them down at night and examining them in the early morning. Formerly 'trets' – long lines with as many as fifty baited hooks on each – were stretched across Broad or river, and many good eels were

Plate 28: *Setting Up the Bow-Net* (LLNB XVIII)
We came across these two old Broadmen setting up their bow-net on a bank near an old broken-down boat-house, hidden from the Broad by a clump of trees. The bow-net is an ingenious contrivance for capturing fish, as the reader will see from my colleague's description. The nets are weighted by stones, and sunk in the swims made by the fish in the weeds. These waterways

taken. This method is now illegal, only a single hook being allowed on any set line.

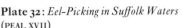

Plate 32: *Eel-Picking in Suffolk Waters* (PEAL XVII)

After the fishing season is over, at the end of December, the Southwold fishermen, when not shrimping, fill up their time by eel-picking, net-making and mending, and sundry other jobs. It is often impossible for them to go out on the cold North Sea at such times, for nothing is to be got there save rough weather. Another reason why the eel-picker defers his sport till winter is the difficulty, nay, almost impossibility, of getting any eels in summer, for they 'fly' during the summer, that is, they leave the mud, and are vagrants in the dykes, swimming hither and thither. The pick, as shown in the plate, is a picturesque tool, not unworthy of the sons of Neptune. It is generally made by the local blacksmith for the modest sum of five shillings, the fir staff, however, costing extra. This particular pick is locally called a 'gall-pick'. It will be seen that it consists of two barbed metal prongs placed between two other rough-hewn prongs. There are, besides this pick, various kinds in use in different parts of England. The experienced eel-picker generally chooses a quiet day, because there will be no ripples on the water, and a morning light, so that he may distinguish the 'blow-holes'. Shouldering his eel-pick, he strides across the common to the dykes, and, walking slowly along the edge of one of them, he looks carefully under the banks for 'blows'. A 'blow' is a round hole with a circlet of blue, much the colour of ink, round it, its size depending on the size of the eel. Each eel has two blows, separated from each other by the length of the eel they harbour. Here it seems the eel lies buried during the cold weather, the blows evidently being his breathing-holes. If the eel-picker can see the two blows, he strikes his pick with a quick movement as nearly as possible between the two holes, whereas, if he can only see one hole, he must take his chance, and, if he strikes wrongly, the eel will depart by the distal end. All these blows are under water. Sometimes the pick will bring up the eel coiling all around its teeth like a 'wiper', at others, it will come up hanging stiffly and oscillating slightly, while at others it will be quite dead and flaccid, due, we should think, to the prongs having penetrated the brain. When the eel comes up, the man rubs his pick up and down on the grass to rub off his slippery prey, which often instinctively glides towards the dyke, but is stopped by a death-blow from a stick. As in other sports, the eel-catcher's luck is subject to great variations. He may get none at all, or he may get two stones of eels in a day, but an average catch for a good day's work is one stone of eels.

Plate 33: *The Haunt of the Pike* (LLNB XV)

There are, as all anglers know, several ways of taking this fish. Our keeper has been snapping – that is, he has strung a small dead roach on to a piece of wire armed with hooks and weighted with leads: he then paddles gently up to an opening in the lilies or the rush, and drops in the bait, pulling it this way or that towards the surface, thus often attracting the hungry fish. In the picture the keeper has secured a four-pound fish, and he is in the act of landing him with his net. But there was a fierce death-struggle first amid the lily-stalks, for these small fish fight harder than the larger, the captive now making for the mud, now entangling the line around a mass of lily-root, now shooting here, now there, but all in vain – the knowing angler has foiled all his manoeuvres, and brings him exhausted to the surface.

Plate 34: *A Marsh Farm* (LLNB XXIX)

A marsh farm is a characteristic sight in East Norfolk, and our plate shows a very typical and picturesque specimen. These small farms vary in size from twenty to a hundred acres, their average rental being two pounds sterling an acre, the grazing lands commanding a sovereign more. The marshes round the farm buildings have no hedges, but are divided by dykes, which are from five to ten feet wide. The larger water-divisions are called swims. At times a drove of cattle may be seen swimming across these, following their leader, who has been carried across in a ferry-boat. The drainage of the marshes, and the natural grasses growing thereon, have been touched upon elsewhere.

Plate 35: *A Toad in the Path – Early Spring in Norfolk* (PEAL XXVII)

The Norfolk cottages are far prettier than any of the cottages in the other Eastern Counties, judging from those we have seen. In Cambridgeshire the cottages did not please us; in Suffolk they are solid and heavy, like the people. The cottages given in our plates are specimens of Norfolk cottages. In one a dyke leads up to the picture. This is not a typical specimen of the Norfolk cottage, but of the transition period from the artistic work of old master-bricklayers to the 'penny-bank' architecture of the modern builders. This one is solidly built of stone, and, now that it is time-stained, is not ugly. On the left of the dyke two little cottage-urchins have spied a toad in their path, and they have stopped to eye the jewelled creature, which has been enticed out on to the grass by the spring warmth.

Plate 36: *The First Frost* (LLNB XIV)

After breaking a channel to the shore, we started to look for pictures, and came across this little nook. This deserted corner was evidently a busier place in summer-time. It is typical of the cottage garden-ends which abut on the Broads. To the left is a reed fence, over the top of which peep a few tassled crests of this year's reed crop, not yet cut; beyond the fence is a small alder carr, the occasional hiding-place of a pheasant or waterfowl. Close by lie several bundles of faggots piled up for winter use, and now partially hidden by the snow. To the right are two boats, one pulled out high and dry and the other frozen in. Beyond extends a thin border of reed, from the other side of which the Broad stretches to the opposite shore. In the right of the plate peeps the beginning of a foot-bridge which leads across a little dyke. Shortly after we had secured this plate a picturesque old man appeared, and with trembling hands drew some of the faggots from under the snow, cut them up, and carried them home.

Plate 37: *A Winter's Morning* (PLFF I)

Plate 38: *A Slippery Path – Winter Scene* (Norfolk) (PEAL XXIII)
The cottages in our plate are tenanted by peasants more prosperous than some we know; yet even here what a life! The scanty cubic space filled with air poisoned with the organic exhalations of the eight human beings we saw sitting in the one room, where the hard-worked mother, dragged down by penury and child-bearing, was preparing a coarse meal for the delicate children, each of whom was suffering from eczema. Pure air and good food they needed, and neither could they get. Unconscious of their grinding fate, they raised to us their large blue serious eyes full of innocent wonder. The day was bitingly cold, but we were glad to get out once more into the air, and escape from that ill-smelling dwelling.

In our plate we see the young mother crossing a slippery ice-glazed plank which bridges the frozen dyke. She, careless of her health, has come from the close house to call her husband, who is busy in the work-shop, to his dinner. He too has been ill with fever and cough-racking bronchitis, which subtly and slowly was block-ing up the paths of his life with its viscid gum. Thanks to the rude doctoring of the village leech, he still lives on, and is now at work.

Plate 39: *Going to Market – A Winter Scene* (PLFF XV)

Plate 40: *A Spring Idyl* (PLFF III)

Plate 41: *Haymaker with Rake* (PEAL XXXI)
From a superficial examination of the Norfolk peasant we find two predominating types; the commoner being men of average height, with rather small massive heads, high cheek-bones, dark bright eyes, and black hair. These men are very active, intelligent, and wiry. The other type is of larger muscular development, with light or reddish hair and grey or blue eyes. These also are good workers, and, though not so active as the smaller men, are mentally superior to them. Both here and in Suffolk the smallness of the hands and feet is very noticeable. In the plate of the haymaker resting we have a speci-men of the smaller dark type of peasant. The marsh-hay has been cut, and he has been sent with others on a threatening afternoon to rake it into cocks, lest the coming rainstorm should wet it during the night. He has nearly done his work, and is resting on his rake. Behind him the marsh is dotted with haycocks; before him, in the distance, stretches the broad, across which he can just see his cottage-home silhouetted against the sky. His face and the haycocks are softly lighted up by the setting sun, which is nearly clouded over by the coming storm.

Plate 42: *A Garden End* (Suffolk) (PEAL XXIX)
Our appetites, though sharpened by our drive, were soon appeased, and we engaged the grinning negro to show us the way to our market-gardener friend, at whose garden we had arranged to meet for some pictures. . . . The garden was beautifully kept, perhaps a little too neatly for our purpose. Carefully pruned and trained apple-trees, loaded with white apple-blossom tinctured with the faintest rosy flush, met us at every turn, while beneath these grew the yellow buds, rosy stalks, and broad green leaves of the rhubarb plant. Lettuces and young onions were springing up from the brown earth, and strong plants of horse-radish grew in rank luxuriance, their biting roots buried deep and cool in the earth. The old gardener – of Hebrew origin – joined us, and pointed exultingly to his spring potatoes, the 'Pride of Hebron', as he had named them with naïve anachronism. He was a venerable old man, with flowing white beard and clear, dark eyes. His face was honest and kindly, and the gentle work of all his life – tending and caring for his plants – seemed to have left its impress on his character.

With pride he pointed to the well-grown fruit trees, bushes, and plants, and then to his two hands, which, he said, had done it all. . . . Presently a charming little girl, also of Jewish lineage, met us, bringing a message from the old gardener. My friend could not keep his eyes off the little Jewess – such a perfect type she was. The kindly old man now led us to his garden-end, the bank of which was brightly coloured with yellow turnip-blossom, which rippled in the breeze. Down the bank grew some exposed roots of horse-radish, ready to be gathered into bundles as required for the market. Blossoming pear-trees grew, trained against the wall, while on a rising bed were picturesque old bell-jars, and frames protecting delicate seedlings of melon and tomato.

We had given the old man one of our cigars, which he smoked with all the ease and enjoyment of an old hand, and when he had finished, he sat down on a low wooden seat and began to pot out a few plants, filling the red pots with rich loamy soil from a rough wooden box. Beside him stood another box full of roots, ready to be potted and go forth on their peaceful and beautiful missions. The young girl, his right hand, as Abraham informed us, stood patiently with her arms full of flower-pots, handing him a fresh one each time he had filled that on which he was employed. There seemed something mystic in the ceremony. Here was this tired old man, at the end of his long life, still working on and setting new plants, destined to live and put forth flowers, and in their turn too to fade and die; sadly he worked, but not complainingly, although he well knew, in all likelihood, he would be dead long before the flowers he was now tending. A gentle breeze was stirring, ruffling the tops of the trees and blowing about the girl's apron. Although evening was falling, it was with difficulty the veteran could be induced to leave his work; but his daughter-in-law persuaded him at last, and as we also were about to return home, he took us warmly by the hand and expressed a hope that he had helped us as we wished. Kind old soul! though he died that summer, he yet lives on, ministering to man's pleasure; by his help to us that day he lives on, still, as he always lived, working to beautify the work-a-day world. The best study of the old man is that in our picture of *The Grafter* (see plate 43), published elsewhere. We afterwards sent his portrait to his son, the only portrait the old man had ever had done, and received in return a letter of deeply-felt gratitude.

Plate 43: *The Grafter* (PLFF VI)

Plate 44: *Furze-Cutting on a Suffolk Common* (PEAL XIII)

Nowhere have we seen furze growing in such luxuriance as on Southwold Common. In spring, when these prickly thickets of sombre green are ablaze with yellow flowers, its full glory is beheld. When we first saw this luxuriant blossoming, its splendour recalled to us the masses of scarlet and white and yellow of tropical flowers; but here, at Southwold, it is the denizen of bleak common and wind-cut field which blooms with all the luxuriance of torrid vegetation.

One day in early autumn we met the intelligent model shown in the plate. He was hard at work with his short stout scythe, cutting the hard wiry stems. We watched him at his work. The stroke is not at all that of the mower, a long, sweeping stroke, but a shorter, sharper stroke, more like the action of cracking a whip. The gorse or furze is generally cut in autumn, so that it may weather or 'sare', as our friend would say, in the autumn sun. He cuts it to keep it down, as otherwise it would soon cover the whole of the common. But even this plant has its uses, and in Suffolk it serves many of the uses to which reed is put in Norfolk. Thus it is required for making sheds for sheep and cattle, and for this purpose it is used green, as in that state it is more easily worked in between the wooden framework. In the green state it is also used for party-walls and the fencing in of cattle-yards, for which purpose it is preferred to anything else, as it keeps the yards very warm. It is used, too, for 'drawing in' to the hurdles during the lambing season. Again, it is employed for building up the river-banks. Bushes of furze are put between piles and the hollows in the bank formed by the tide, and these are then filled up with soft mud, a tenacious cement being thus made.

Plate 45: *In the Barley Harvest* (Suffolk) (PEAL VII)

On our return to the barley-field we determined to take a plate during one of the short rests so frequent in this hard labour. Here one man is honing his scythe, while another, his face streaming with perspiration, has taken off his hat with which to fan himself, and now stretches forth his hand to his mate, who, leaving his rake in the field, has brought the bottle of 'home-brewed' from which they will all quench their thirst. Through the hot day they will work under the broiling summer sun until 4.30 p.m., when they rest and have tea, or 'fourses', as it is now locally called, its name formerly being 'beavers'. After half an hour's grace they again fall to, and work hard till seven in the evening, when it is a common sight to meet gangs of these tired labourers going home with scythes and rakes, empty bottles and baskets, and probably a few rabbits killed that day in the fields.

Plate 46: *Shocking Corn* (Norfolk) (PEAL VIII)
Our second plate shows a harvest-scene on a Norfolk marsh. As a rule, but little wheat is grown on these lowland farms, the soil being better adapted to other crops. Here, however, the marsh-farmer is at work on another part of the marsh, while his two sons shock the corn, one building up the pile, whilst the other brings him the schooves.

Plate 47: *The Clay-Mill* (Norfolk) (PEAL XXI)
Walking on, we came to a picturesque well, whence the workmen drew their water by means of a heavy beam – an old-fashioned method, and one we had not expected to see still in use in the latter part of the nineteenth century. We next went round the standards, and came upon two mills at work, and very beautiful and suggestive were they as one watched the old horse plodding round and round the clay path. The driver and his mate eyed us, and the driver at length politely said, 'Good morning', but the grin was still there, and we wondered what had happened to make every one so jocular.

Plate 48: *The Mangold Harvest* (PLFF IV)

Plate 49A: *A March Pastoral* (Suffolk) (PEAL XII)
Here is depicted, in very early spring, the hedgerow of a Suffolk field. The sombre tone well expresses the bleak, raw day of early March. An old ewe occupies the foreground, with her two young lambs tugging at her full udders, thus already beginning the battle of life. On the hedge itself, a lamb of independent character – he is only two or three weeks old – nibbles at the grass. We have read somewhere that in a certain country (India, we think) the cattle-breeders watch for these independent members of the flock and choose them before others for breeding stock. It is as with men; those who huddle together have but little character; original minds always wander from the flock. In the distance of the picture the lambs lie about on the ground, whilst the ewes search about for delicate morsels of new grass or early budding herb. These sheep are not of pure breed, with the exception, perhaps, of the sheep in the hedgerow, which are of the black-faced Suffolk breed. In this country the lambs are born in the cold fields, and in sheep-yards made with hurdles interlaced with gorse. Inside this yard a pen is made by enclosing a smaller space with furze-panelled hurdles, and roofing it in by placing other hurdles across them. The floor is

littered with straw. When a ewe drops a lamb, the young creature is picked up by the shepherd, who takes it into the pen, and, by imitating the bleating of the lamb, entices the mother in after him. He places the lamb in the warm straw, and leaves both ewe and lamb there for a few hours. The sheep in the picture are nibbling at grass and turnips, which the shepherd has pulled, and cast along the hedgerow to leeward, so that the sheep can feed and the lambs be protected from the biting north-easterly winds so prevalent in March. The lambs' tails have been cut, which points to their age being over a fortnight, for it is the practice to cut their tails and geld them at a fortnight old. Lambs born in the end of February and beginning of March will be ready for killing as fat lambs in July or August. Lamb in some parts of England is very dear, commanding from one shilling to fourteen pence a pound retail; but in this, as well as most other supplies, it is the middle-man who secures the prize.

Plate 49B: *The Bowling Green* (WLTW IX)

Plate 50: *At the Grindstone – A Suffolk Farmyard* (PEAL XXX)
A Suffolk peasant is here sharpening his 'bagging-iron' at the common grindstone, which is being turned by his son. Near the boy is the bucket with which the well-water was brought to make the dry stone work. All around is a crop of nettles, the only produce of the poor soil. To the left rises a pole with a hook, euphoniously called the 'hog-pole', that is, the pole from which pigs are hung to be dressed and cleaned when killed. Beyond the fence stretches the orchard, where the linen is drying and bleaching in the sweet pure air. To the right is a gateway, through which winds a path leading down to the marshes. From the distant hedgerow rise the tall elms, beautiful in form and delicate in touch. Here the peasant is quietly but determinedly sharpening his weapon with which to fight the ever-encroaching bramble, whitethorn, and blackthorn. He does not hurry, but performs his task with quiet, solemn dignity, pressing his weight on the steel blade as the boy with opposing force turns the grindstone.

The farmer whose yard is here depicted is our keen critic already spoken of, and we were interested to hear what he would think of the work of Jean François Millet, peasant and painter; so we showed him some of the reproductions in Sensier's admirable Life. He passed all he understood as being thoroughly 'workman-like'. The vine-dresser he would not criticise, as he said he did not understand it, for he had never seen vine-culture. Now, curiously enough, this farmer found much the same faults with Millet's 'Pig-Killers' as Millet found with a translator of the Idyls of Theocritus – the faults being that neither understood exactly what he wished to express.

Plate 51: *Rope Spinning* (WLTW XIX)

Plate 52: *Osier-Peeling* (Norfolk) (PEAL XIV)
Here we have a basket-maker's yard as seen by us one beautiful day in early spring. Here, at the brakes, we see three women hard at work peeling the pliant osier stems, while the sun glints through the leafless trees and lights up the dark scene. A donkey, all unconscious, is feeding knee-deep in a pile of sweet mucilaginous peelings, and to the right sits a boy trying his 'prentice hand at basket-making. Through the large windows we can see a more experienced hand busy bending the withered rods and fashioning the rough hamper, which we can picture to ourselves, when finished, travelling full of hares and pheasants, wild-fowl and venison, salmon and grouse, from one end of Great Britain to the other. The intelligent 'prentice has seen us, and comes up politely, volunteering to show us everything; so we desire to begin at the beginning, and learn the art and science of basket-making as practised in Norfolk at the present day. The osiers, he told us, were usually cut in April, by regular hands employed for the purpose, whose wage was threepence a bunch, each bunch measuring seventy-two inches round, two bundles measuring thirty-six inches each, making one bundle. The implement used for cutting is a hook. The osiers are grown in small patches on the marshes near the Broads, and in some districts seem to pay better than in others. But we have heard very conflicting evidence from trustworthy men as to the value of osier-cultivation; so much so, that to the present day we are rather mystified as to the real value of such a crop. One thing, however, seems certain, that of late years the supply exceeds the demand. The basket-maker buys the osiers from the farmer for five or six shillings a bunch, or two-and-sixpence to three shillings a bundle, including cartage. When they arrive at the basket-maker's, they are put in a dyke containing a little water, and here they weather, the object of which is to loosen the peel, which facilitates the peeling. We have seen the dyke full of bunches and bundles all sprouting, many

with full-grown leaves, looking like osier-plantations growing in very close quarters. They remain in this bath from April to June. If, however, they are intended for rough use, they never go to the dyke at all, for they are not peeled, but laid out in the sun to dry and 'brown', and the two kinds are always distinguished as 'whites' and 'browns'. To return to the whites, which are used for better wares. After the soaking and growing in the dyke, the bundles are taken out, the lashing cut, and the muddy ends of the osiers washed in a large tub of water standing ready. Then they are carried to the brakes. These are uprights with a narrow slit, at the bottom of which is placed a sharp knife-edge. The operation of peeling is done by placing a single osier rod in the slit, and pulling it quickly and firmly through, the peel falling on one side, the white rod being placed on the operator's right. The peelers get threepence a bundle for their work, and can peel four bundles a day. We have always seen this work done by women and girls, for though requiring steadiness, not much strength is necessary. The old peelings are kept to protect bundles of 'browns' which have 'weathered' and are ready for the basket-maker. The whites are carefully put into sheds until required.

Plate 53: *The Basket Maker* (Norfolk) (PEAL XV)
The rods are used for making swills, baskets, skeps (troughs for feeding bullocks), cradles, and perambulators. The basket-maker, who works either in a covered shed or in an open one according to the weather, sits on a board on the ground; his chief tool is a short broad-bladed knife, sharp as a razor. Simple as a basket looks when made, it does not look such easy work as one watches the smart workman picking his osiers from seven assorted sizes, and bending the twigs to their proper places, cutting here and there, and twirling the basket round first this way, then that. He works hard, and considers he has done a good day's work when he has made a dozen common hampers and lids, large enough to hold a good-sized cod or salmon. For these he will get three shillings; and surely he will have earned every penny of it, for considerable skill is required; for besides the actual knowledge of basket-making, there is great judgment needed for using the appropriate osiers at the right time. Such hampers sell for eightpence each.

The basket-maker whom we see at work in the second plate was as obliging as his son, who was learning the trade, and entered well into the spirit of the thing when we suggested a picture; so we wish him a long life and a great sale of baskets, swills, and skeps, but we are not sure we wish as great a demand for his cradles and perambulators.

Plate 54: *A Dame's School* (PLFF II)

Plate 55: *The Stickleback Catcher* (PLFF XVI)

Plate 56: *Confessions* (PLFF V)

Plate 57: *A Fisherman at Home* (PLFF XX)

Plate 58: *A Yarmouth Row* (WLTW XXV)

Plate 59: *In a Sail-Loft* (WLTW XVIII)

Plate 60: *The Poacher* (PLFF XI)

Plate 61: *The Poacher – A Hare in View* (Suffolk) (PEAL II)
In our first plate, the poacher, with his lurcher, is working on a common surrounded by dykes. His mate has netted the gates, and in the early morning light he is holding his dog, whilst he watches a hare which is running straight for the net.

Plate 62: *A Stiff Pull* (Suffolk) (PEAL IV)
Our plate shows us a stiff pull, such as is life for many. Like the horses and the ploughman in the plate, they must look neither to the right nor to the left, but straight before them, putting all their strength into their work. Slowly they climb the steep ascent of years, and finally, when they have reached the top, they sink down exhausted under the disappointments of life's imperfections. But this honest peasant, a true son of Suffolk, dogged, grasping, not over intelligent, and rather boorish, little recks he of such thoughts. Enough if he keeps off the 'rheumatics', and has bacon and bread and beer to satisfy his appetite.

Plate 63: *At Plough – The End of the Furrow* (PLFF XIII)

Plate 64: *Decayed Fishermen* (WLTW XII)

Appendixes

References and Bibliography

BIBLIOGRAPHY

PICTORIAL BOOKS

Life and Landscape on the Norfolk Broads (with T. F. Goodall), 1886. Illustrated with forty platinotypes.

Idyls of the Norfolk Broads, 1886. Illustrated with twelve autogravure plates.

Pictures from Life in Field and Fen, 1887. Illustrated with twenty photogravure plates.

Pictures of East Anglian Life, 1888. Illustrated with thirty-two photo-etchings.

Wild Life on a Tidal Water (with T. F. Goodall), 1890. Illustrated with thirty-one photo-etchings.

On English Lagoons, 1893.

Birds, Beasts and Fishes of the Norfolk Broadland, 1895.

Marsh Leaves, 1895. Illustrated with sixteen photo-etchings.

A SELECT LIST OF EMERSON'S OTHER PUBLICATIONS

Paul Ray at the Hospital : a picture of student life, 1882.

Naturalistic Photography for Students of the Art, 1889. Second edition, 1890. Third edition, revised, 1899.

Mrs Cameron, photographs by Mrs J. M. Cameron with a descriptive essay by P. H. Emerson, 1889.

English Idyls, 1889.

The Death of Naturalistic Photography, 1890.

East Coast Yarns, 1891.

Notes on Perspective Drawing and Vision, 1891.

A Son of the Fens, 1892.

Signor Lippo, Burnt-Cork Artiste, 1893.

Tales from Welsh Wales, 1894.

Welsh Fairy Tales, 1894.

Caóba, the Guerilla Chief, 1897.

The English Emersons, 1898.

Suggested Amended Billiard Rules for Amateur Players, 1908.

The Emersons alias Embersons of Ipswich, 1912.

The Blood Eagle and Other Tales, 1925.

REFERENCES

1. T. R. Dallmeyer, *The Photogram*, 1899, p. 354.
2. *The Amateur Photographer*, 19 March 1886, pp. 138–9.
3. *The Amateur Photographer*, 9 April 1886, p. 176.
4. Ibid.
5. *Pictorial Effect in Photography*, 1869, p. 109.
6. *Naturalistic Photography*, 1889, p. 23.
7. Ibid., p. 25.
8. Ibid., p. 31.
9. Ibid., pp. 255–6.
10. Ibid., p. 150.
11. *Photographic News*, 3 May 1889, p. 289.
12. *Photographic News*, 7 June 1889, p. 380.
13. *British Journal of Photography*, 6 September 1889, p. 595.
14. *British Journal of Photography*, 30 August 1889.
15. *Photographic Art Journal*, 2 June 1890, p. 100.
16. *Photographic Art Journal*, 1 August 1890, p. 142.
17. *The Photogram*, 1899, p. 347.
18. *The Emerson's alias Emberson's* Book IV, p. 15, privately published, 1923.
19. *Naturalistic Photography*, p. 214.

Emerson Medallists

In 1925 I offered artistic silver and bronze medals, executed by the late J. Havard Thomas, a most distinguished sculptor, who excelled at low-relief work. The conditions were printed in the Photographic Press. Nationality had no influence and nothing but artistic merit of the prints submitted counted. Twelve was the minimum number of prints demanded. The results were printed in the *British Journal* up to 1930. A few have been added since, for many very old prints became accessible in 1931.

Silver Medals

1. Hippolyte Bayard (French), 1839, for pictorial photographs and for inventing a process of taking photographs and for having first exhibited publicly pictorial photographs (in Paris) in 1839.
2. An unknown French photographer in Paris, 1865, for an unknown lady with a cigarette.
3. W. Türck (Dane), for figure-subjects, children out of doors, and interiors, 1908.
4. H. G. Ponting (English) for artistic stereographs in war and peace.
5. Julie Lourberg (Dane), for studio portraits, especially of children and architecture.
6. P. Lewis (English), for instantaneous landscapes.
7. Captain D. English (English), for artistic natural history photographs.
8. Karl 'Klic', painter (Bohemian), 1875, for having invented the photo-aquatint process and done many plates in the process.
9. E. Drummond Young (Scot), for portraits and his excellent text book on the subject.

1 & 2. O. Hill and Adamson (Scots), 1842, for calotype portraits only.
3. S. Buckle (English), for landscapes and a figure-subject (calotype), 1858.
4. Louis Pierson (French), 1855. The actress Elise Félix ('Rachel').
5. Gaspard Félix Tournachon, 'Nadar' (French), Racine's Vine and interview with Chevreul, the colour savant, 1860.
6. The quarter Kleine Fleet at Hamburg, 1860, by an unknown Hamburg photographer.
7. Julia M. Cameron (English), 1864–70, for portraits only.
8. Captain Cromer (French) for portraits and landscapes.
9. N. Perscheid (German), for portraits and open-air figure-subjects.
10. Dr E. B. Goodwin (Swede), for portraits only.
11. W. A. Cadby (English), for children's portraits and alpines.
12. R. Craig Annan (Scot), for the excellence of his photo-aquatints.
13. T. Bolas, F.I.C., F.C.S. (English), for his accurate learning and honest contributions to photographic journalism and for his invention of the hand camera.
14. Minna Keene (English), for her pictorial photos, landscapes, interiors and figure-subjects.
15. Miss Gad (Dane), for her studio portraits of children and architecture.
16. Colonel Noverre (English), for pictorial 'pin-holes'.
17. E. H. Atkinson (English), for his excellent untouched half-tone blocks.
18. W. L. Colls (English), for the excellence of his photo-aquatint plates.

To complete the awards under *the old regulations* we have awarded medals to the following: SILVER to Col. Nicéphore de Niépce (French), for the invention of photography. Rev. J. B. Reade, M.A., F.R.S. (English) for having invented the calotype process and hypo fixer. Charles Victor Hugo (French) for the photograph of Vaquere's cat, taken at Jersey when in exile. W. Carleman (Swede), a painter, for the letterpress half-tone block, 1870. BRONZE, Sabatier Blot (French) for portraits, 1842. Le Sec (French) for landscape and still life. Dr D. O. H. Fielitz (German), court-physician to the King of Prussia, for portraits. R. Fenton (English) for the Russian battery at Sevastopol after its capture by the British. H. Biow (German) for portraits. Braun of Dornach (German) for flowers. William Green (English) for being the first to photograph nesting birds in their natural surroundings, 1881–6. W. H. Harrison (English) for inventing the gelatinobromide dry plate and pyro developer. R. A. Bennet (English) for having invented the *rapid* gelatino-bromide dry plate. Peter Maudsley (English) for inventing bromide printing paper. W. Willis (?) for inventing the platinotype process. Sir J. Swan, F.R.S. (English), for having invented the *transfer method* in carbon printing. J. M. Whitehead (Scot) for landscapes, fruit and flowers. Dr L. Mees, S. H. Wratten and J. Cadett (all English) for the advancement of the process of panchromatic photography. T. R. Dallmeyer (English) for the telephoto lens. R. Eickmeyer (United States) for having founded pictorial photography in the U.S.A. (at Yonkers), and for his artistic photo, 'On the shoals at Bargenat (N.J.)'. J. Ross by W. Richmond (English) for the telecentric lens. Simpson, M.A., English (Cantab.) for the chloride of silver printing paper. F. Judge (English) for landscapes. F. Colman (United States) artist, for a series of Capri photos. Fréchon (French), of Basra, for a series of French cottage interiors, published in *Country Life*. ************ (Scot), of Christorphon, N.B., for a series of small instantaneous landscapes. Villon de Villeneuve (French) for portraits of the actors and actresses of the Comédie Française, 1853–5 (calotypes). Brassai, Paris, for night photography, *Paris de nuit. This closes the awards under the old regulations.*

P. H. Emerson, B.A., M.B. (Cantab.)
'Elmo'
3 Avenue Road
Falmouth, Cornwall
Oct. 7th 1933